from out here in space
earth is rising
cities are illuminated
forests green
oceans blue

no alien life
only ones i love

"christmas past"

bitter chilled morning
jack leaves his frosted swirl on window
sylvia tells me to go to sleep so
christmas will come
but i want to see
tired eyes droop and blink and close

...suddenly it was morning and pillowcases at the end of the
bed bulged with
books, more books
a small typewriter, puzzles and games, and a doll
no screams from us
breathless delight

we run to mam n da
HE CAME we yell
they all sleep eye and sandman
roll us in covers
read this da
sez i
gruff voice begins

"mole thought his happiness complete when...."

we were complete
maybe the last christmas we ever were

"chrrrristmass"

rum tum tiddle
rum tum taw
nothing like an irish christmas
truth be told
christmas don't need irish
and irish don't need christmas
at all, at all
a swirl and fiddle
a twirl an irish riddle
tap yer feet
slap yer knee
then drink
to you and me
rum tum tiddle
rum tum taw

"ground breaks"

i fell
drifting through planets and stars
moon over my shoulder
sun in my eyes

what i wanted was a catcher
a soft landing
but here only ghosts
translucent hands held out to grip

you said its hard to let go
and hold on
true story

falling still through ink
then the poet speaks
each phrase births a new planet
every word forms a shooting star

good he is
and lost

planet waves ripple
bending light into white rainbows
while somewhere over...
those shooting stars
well
they found their mark
true story

black and white
all color bled out
white and black...
and where they meet
dark
blood
red

(dec 2013)

it's the eve
and Christmas waits
drinking begun
shopping done
and still Christmas waits
presents are wrapped
glasses tapped
Christmas waits
somewhere on this star
the glory of it all
waits for us
so lets slow and remember
love is the reason

"sad songs"

i need some music babe
some mellow and sorta sad...

you played
toussaint and miles

hathaway, billie too

nothing takes the place
words true
sooner or later nothing seems the same
so i wait
for...

soft sax low brass
down and blue
floating notes like rafts
piano plays a chord or two
still waiting

been so many places
and what i hope to be
darlin' can't you see
if no words come together
then play
piano ripples down and slow
enter strings
a song for you

when you're alone
the magic dies
no sunrise
lonely hours with
faded memories

you played
filled all the hollow notes
filled mellow and sad
yeah bb
you knew
i needed some bad

"littered life"

growing up
11 and counting back in sometime and times of some
knew i was gonna be...this side of kandinsky
12 let in some doubt 'cos times were a changing
and fathers were dying
unlucky 13
no da
no ma to speak of
lost not found
(you know that shit)
broken hearts littered the floor

still painting
14 discovered rock n roll, fast bikes, and ...
fast

still painting
skip a few and here we are at 18
looking for me and finding you
yet came a time traveling to foreign lands
and foreign loves
took dylan
lived his songs
killed 'em good
lost you
found me

husbands came and went
lovers too
littered floors remained littered
with bleeding hearts and unpainted canvas
the leading lady swooned as
dylan sang
blood on tracks
and buckets of tears
the i gave myself a good talking to...

still painting

and here i am
grown up, getting old
still on this side of kandinsky
still littering floors
still living, still loving
still painting
still talking to myself

"aloe"

he caused a scene
be careful said M
and i, not listening
i went my way
now i'm not your lover
and you are not the one

cellos play
don't break hearts they said
lies become the truth
and violins play
truth is beaten down
cymbals clash

i'm not your lover
and though i lost my way
i found home
you
are
not
the
one

(undertow)

i sailed faraway across rippled sand
under indian stars and winter moon
hidden behind a blackened veil
blinded eyes and shattered heart
i roamed these deserts in search of ....
a familiar
a like spirit
oh i believed in you
i thought you were truth
a foundling love
a precious vessel
a heart of silver and gold

but diamond eyes and crocodile tears glittered sharp
and speared the silver that was my heart
the voice
yes the very same that once crooned soft
that voice now throws its barb
and cuts deep
and lies ruined a crumbled fortress

(the mirage of clear sweet water)
the truth revealed
a murky undertow neath stagnant green

where am i ?
a wraith still wandering darkened dunes
lost and thirsty
a trail of sand behind long shadow
one step more and another
and another

(once more)

somewhere across the ocean
beneath a lowering sky
two islands strung together
the land of the long white cloud

an old love
a memory held close
never forgot you baby
flash of blue eyes
replay in my head
boyish grin still makes me smile

i think of how we were
and wonder where you are
and if you ever think of me

somewhere along a coast of clouded isles
mirrored in glistening blue
a piece of my heart still skips a beat
at the memory of you

"poet beanie"

hats are like extra
voices in head
held in by baseball and beanie

church going
wedding showing
racetrack posing
hard hat dozing

my hat
lets no words out
until invited by blank page
or unprimed canvas
then..a sunlit river gushes
i need a sunhat

"making word play"

guitar gentle chords
(not plucked)
splayed fingers strum
a concerto including wind and reed

drink up baby
your hands in the air
and comets swoop through ink

we be here in dark thoughts
in night
stabbed in the chest
but gentle like

don't day...please don't break
strident light shrieks
draw the curtains
pour another
and together
we be here

"what's on your mind?"

you should be here
with me
so where are you?

you make me smile
deep in your words and chords
you make me happy

like bees on ...
bzzzzing
nectar making
honey

here's what i say
don't think i can
without

know i can't
even tho
these words you write
speak different

you make me smile

"after life"

bottle of cabernet
seven oaks it said
which seven? i wonder if still there
silhouetted 'gainst twilit sky
could be only six
six wondering why
five ?
as one leaves
red and gold then cold
four so unsure how
one could die
and like
father, son and holy ghost
three oaks stand tall
spirit spirited
left and leaved

"outside the lines"

brown man...well
cafe au lait in truth
wrote 8
with a million words and one more
spoke three (i love you)
and three million more

a dictionary of misspelled words
cast spells
intent made sure

grammar punctured
but he's a
grammar phone of soul music
invented language...run ons and run downs
poems and prose
subtle smiles and clouded frowns
thrown down nonchalant gestures
played to affect

could be cinnamon
his color could be nutmeg
or spiced, seasoned with heat
pure mystery
can someone explain
a brown poet

(blue screen)

a tv in a room distant
plays melancholy music
while actors star in tragic roles

in this room
more music
a backdrop to
words of sad and lonely
slipping across waves and drowned

tv wails
oh darling nothing takes the place
nothing takes the place of you

when morning breaks
my blue heart breaks too

back here in real time
shreds of emotion remain
the thread that was unravels
and ...
lies disentangle from bitter lips

nothing takes the place

"chilled out"

if i make you crazy cos i'm faster
you could speed up
it's cold outside

warmer in

but when you're slow
i try to chill
n sometimes i'm an ice floe
and you're the titanic
no icebreaker you
you're sinking under cold seas
deeper than i can dive
then mermaids drag you down

i could do this again
start over
fish the ocean for you
if you let me
i could be a warm breeze
on a cold night

"bitter"

same shit
unplugged
alternate version
gonna love this

acoustic driving
listening and breathing
turned into something of the heart

a chorus of angels sing
it's coming to an end
i'm not your lover
i'm not your friend

hope i can forgive
hope we can make amends
carving worlds from words

"strummed"

what's the matter with me
nope no
at the bottom
a cool place to be
guitar and words
somethin' bout the words

this guy comes with song
and words and more words
and yes
yep
at the top
words and guitar
i hope you will do this for me

shot in the heart
the best silver bullet
strummed and hummed
and laid me down to rest
looking for ghosts
hoped you would do this for me
better than a kiss

(tuesday)

QUIT FUCKING AROUND you said
WRITE you said
you knew the pretty from the mess i couldn't see
caught in this trap

then you made paper figures from news print
and i made print
so here we are
wrote and figured
while sam cooke brought sweet loving
home to me

"how to be a poet"

play me some more music
you can do that
you jumped off
and i followed
fell but not down
just falling

these words for what they mean
are tattoo'd ink black
flamed heat rising
seared and ashed

then a first note
cooled and cool
crooned words

and here we are
stung

"imagine"

solitary dance
a stringed crescendo
internal music of heart(s)
an imaginary lover
laid head on shoulder
whisper of warm breathe

i wonder where you are
if only

worlds could collide
we would meet
somewhere near or ?
in the middle

so here we dance
translucent steps across night skies
what'll i do
with all these stars

i keep you in my pocket
stars to come out soon
light the way
meet me in the middle
lets dance to blue moons

Printed in Great Britain
by Amazon

51634738R00019